Sports Illustrated KIDS

Traditions and Superstitions

FOOTBALL'S *Best* TRADITIONS *and* WEIRDEST SUPERSTITIONS

by Elliott Smith

CAPSTONE PRESS
a capstone imprint

Published by Capstone Press, an imprint of Capstone
1710 Roe Crest Drive, North Mankato, Minnesota 56003
capstonepub.com

Library of Congress Cataloging-in-Publication Data
Names: Smith, Elliott, 1976- author.
Title: Football's best traditions and weirdest superstitions / by Elliott Smith.
Description: North Mankato, Minnesota : Capstone Press, 2023. | Series: Sports illustrated kids. Traditions and superstitions | Includes bibliographical references and index. | Audience: Ages 8-11 | Audience: Grades 4-6 | Summary: "Going to a football game? Wish the players on the latest Madden NFL game cover a little extra luck. And see if you can spot the 12th Man at a Texas A&M game-they should be easy to find. But first, gear up to discover the ins and outs of good fun and good luck in football. With engaging text and striking photos, this book will delight young sports fan with some of the best and weirdest practices on the field and in the stands"-- Provided by publisher.
Identifiers: LCCN 2022013051 (print) | LCCN 2022013052 (ebook) |
ISBN 9781666346862 (hardcover) | ISBN 9781666346893 (pdf) | ISBN 9781666346916 (kindle edition)
Subjects: LCSH: Football--Miscellanea--Juvenile literature. | Superstition--Juvenile literature.
Classification: LCC GV950.7 .S587 2023 (print) | LCC GV950.7 (ebook) | DDC 796.330973--dc23/eng/20220502
LC record available at https://lccn.loc.gov/2022013051
LC ebook record available at https://lccn.loc.gov/2022013052

Editorial Credits
Editor: Ericka Smith; Designer: Tracy Davies; Media Researcher: Svetlana Zhurkin; Production Specialist: Katy LaVigne

Image Credits
Alamy: Reuters/Ben Nelms, 19, ZUMA Press/The Palm Beach Post/Allen Eyestone, 10, ZUMA Wire/Minneapolis Star Tribune/Carlos Gonzalez, 23 (middle); Associated Press: Al Messerschmidt, 26, David Stluka, 29, File/Todd Ponath, 9, National Football League/Ed Rieker, 27; Dreamstime: Robert Philip, 14; Getty Images: Emilee Chinn, 7, Michael Reaves, 13; Newscom: Cal Sport Media/Patrick Green, 11, Icon Sportswire/David Stacy, 16, Icon Sportswire/Russell Lansford, 17, ZUMA Press/Monica Herndon, 15; Shutterstock: DGIM studio (burst background), cover and throughout, Emilio100, 18, Joseph Sohm, 4, Mott Jordan, cover (title fonts), Mtsaride (football), cover and throughout, Nerthuz, cover (bottom left), Sergiy Kuzmin, 23 (top), Steve Jacobson, 28, Svetlana Bayanova, cover (top left), Tony Baggett, 23 (bottom), v74, 22 (top), Venus Angel, cover (bottom middle), wacpan, cover (bottom right), 20, xpixel (colorful candy), cover; Sports Illustrated: Al Tielemans, 21, Erick W. Rasco, 5, 22 (bottom), 25

All internet sites appearing in back matter were available and accurate when this book was sent to press.

Direct Quotations
Page 11, from November 23, 2021, ESPN article, "Thanksgiving Day Games History: Why the Lions and Cowboys Play Every Year, Best Moments, Traditions, Records," espn.com

Page 20, from October 2, 2019, ESPN article, "Meet Tom Brady's Most Trusted Teammate: His 1995 Shoulder Pads," espn.com

Page 23, from October 2, 2019, ESPN article, "Tabasco Shots, Baths, and Gross Gloves: The Best Rituals and Superstitions on All 32 NFL Teams," espn.com

Printed and bound in the USA. 4882

TABLE OF CONTENTS

Words in **bold** are in the glossary.

GOING DEEP

Football can be played almost anywhere. It only takes a few friends and a ball to start the action. No matter where a game starts up, traditions are everywhere. Maybe old friends play at their favorite local park. Maybe a group of college students plays every year during spring break. From high school games to the pros, traditions help make football fun.

THE BIG GAME

The Super Bowl, one of the biggest football traditions, began in 1967. It has become well known for the exciting competition, the amazing halftime shows, and the entertaining commercials that air during the game.

CHAPTER 1

NFL TRADITIONS

The National Football League (NFL) is the most popular sports league in the United States. Every year millions of fans watch their games. As the NFL grew, so did the game's traditions. In between the hard hits and **Hail Marys**, keep an eye out for the unique traditions of teams and fans.

A TERRIBLE TRADITION

In 1975, Pittsburgh Steelers radio announcer Myron Cope had an idea for a playoff game. He thought fans could wave a simple towel to show their support for the team. Cope wasn't sure his idea would work, but on the day of the game, more than 30,000 fans waved their Terrible Towels. A tradition was born.

The Terrible Towel is now a major symbol for the Steelers. Wherever the team plays, the Terrible Towel is sure to be found.

Steelers fans have even taken their towels with them outside the stadium! The Terrible Towel has traveled to the Great Wall of China. It has also made it to Mount Everest and the International Space Station!

LEAP OF FAITH

Nothing is more exciting than scoring a touchdown. For players, it's payoff for their hard work. For fans, it's a chance to praise their team.

At Green Bay's Lambeau Field, the two combine for a signature celebration. The first Lambeau Leap happened in 1993. Defensive back LeRoy Butler scored a touchdown on a **fumble**. Then he jumped into the first row of stands. Fans surrounded him in celebration. After that, Packers players began leaping into the stands after scoring.

Sometimes, an opposing team's player will attempt a Lambeau Leap. But Packers fans show them their disapproval. They push them out of the stands.

LeRoy Butler celebrates with a Lambeau Leap during a 1995 game against the Cincinnati Bengals.

TURKEY AND FOOTBALL

For NFL fans, Thanksgiving is a special day—
football and food take center stage. The tradition
started because the Detroit Lions wanted to
increase their popularity with fans. Since 1934,
the Lions have played on the holiday almost
every year. They didn't play for a few years
during World War II.

A 2006 Thanksgiving Day game between the Lions and
the Miami Dolphins

In 1966, the Dallas Cowboys joined the tradition. And in 2006, the league added a third game. But that game has no specific **host** team, so its location changes. Detroit and Dallas fans, though, will always be able to attend the game and then hurry home for Thanksgiving dinner.

"My favorite thing about playing on Thanksgiving is we're the only team playing at that time, all eyes on us," said Cowboys running back Ezekiel Elliott.

LUCKY NO. 12

There are only 11 players on the field for each team, but some teams have really passionate fans they consider

a twelfth player. The Seattle Seahawks have retired the No. 12 because of their fans. The idea of a 12th Man actually started in 1922 at Texas A&M University. The football coach asked a student athlete in the stands, E. King Gill, to join the team in case he needed to fill in for a player on a badly injured team. He stood on the sidelines ready to help the team, but didn't have to play. Now Texas A&M University students stand during football games to support their team.

CHAPTER 2

COLLEGE TRADITIONS

College football fans are wild about their schools. Students and **alumni** feel a special connection with their universities, so college traditions make Saturdays an action-packed day of sports and celebration.

THE TURNOVER CHAIN

Making a big play is worthy of a sweet reward. The University of Miami was looking for a way to motivate their defense to create more turnovers. In 2017, they came up with the Turnover Chain. When players create a turnover, they're awarded the chain on the sideline. This sets off a huge celebration.

Amari Carter (right) celebrates an interception with the Turnover Chain.

The first version of the shiny piece of jewelry was shaped liked Miami's logo. It was filled with orange and green sapphires.

Other schools created similar rewards. The University of Akron awards its players the Takeaway Pencil. And Boise State University had a Turnover **Throne**.

BAND BATTLES

One of the coolest traditions at Historically Black Colleges and Universities (HBCUs) is seeing the marching bands perform.

Schools like Florida A&M University and Southern University have amazing bands. They can play classic compositions and today's hits. That makes halftime a must-watch event during their games. Sometimes the halftime show is more important than the game!

The fun continues after the game. Some schools take part in the Fifth Quarter. During this event, the opposing bands have a musical battle.

THE WORLD'S BIGGEST DRUM?

Since 1921, Purdue University's band equipment has included what it claims is the largest drum in the world. The drum's actual size is kept secret because there's competition from other college bands with big drums. But in 2021, a Purdue spokesperson estimated that it's about 10 feet (3 meters) tall, on wheels, and weighs about 565 pounds (256 kilograms).

Florida A&M University's band performs during a 2017 game.

AMAZING ENTRANCES

As the home team takes the field before a game, some colleges plan **elaborate** entrances. This helps get fans fired up.

At the University of Oklahoma, two ponies rocket out of the tunnel pulling a covered wagon called the Sooner Schooner.

At Georgia Tech, a 1930 Ford Model A is the mascot. The car, nicknamed the Ramblin' Wreck, has led the football team out to the field since 1961.

University of Oklahoma's Sooner Schooner

At the University of Colorado, a live buffalo named Ralphie leads the charge onto the field. Ralphie V weighed about 1,200 pounds (544 kg)!

University of Colorado's Ralphie with his runners

JUMP AROUND!

"Jump Around" has become the official anthem of the University of Wisconsin. Between the third and fourth quarters, fans jump for the entire length of the song.

CHAPTER 3

PLAYER SUPERSTITIONS

The best football players use skill and smarts to succeed. But for some, there's also a bit of luck involved. Many players have superstitions they think help them on the field. In a sport as hard as football, they certainly can't hurt.

CANDY CRUSH

Former running back Marshawn Lynch always had a sweet tooth. When he was a child, his mom would give him Skittles before football games. It would help with his nerves. This practice seemed to help Lynch play well, so eating Skittles became part of his routine throughout college.

Lynch throws Skittles at fans during a 2014 parade to celebrate the Seattle Seahawks' Super Bowl win.

After he joined the NFL, Lynch ate Skittles after scoring touchdowns. He even wore a custom pair of Skittles **cleats**. Fans also threw him bags of Skittles from the stands. And Lynch eventually became a spokesperson for the candy.

WELL-WORN PADS

Legendary quarterback Tom Brady has won seven Super Bowl games. With all the success he has had, it's hard to imagine he is superstitious.

But Brady does have one superstition. It has lasted more than two decades. In 1995, while at the University of Michigan, Brady was assigned shoulder pads. He liked them so much that he kept using them. Every year he would get them fixed. But he never changed the pads.

"I've worn them for 25 years," Brady said. "Once you find something you like, you stick with it."

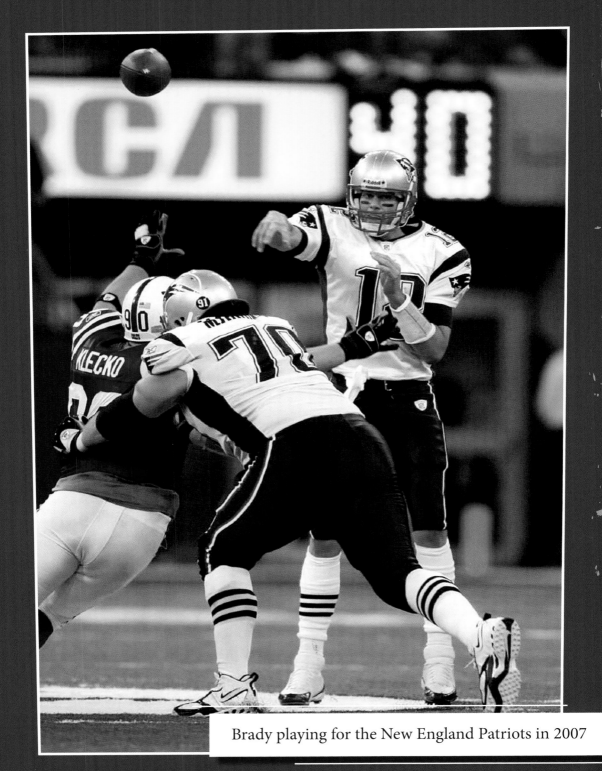

Brady playing for the New England Patriots in 2007

VIDEO GAME PREVIEW

It's no secret that NFL players love playing John Madden video games. But receiver Emmanuel Sanders takes it one step further. Before every game, Sanders takes control of his team in the video game. He plays against the team he will face in real life. He must beat the team in the video game to feel good about his chances in real life.

Sanders (left) in a 2021 game against the New York Jets

HOT IN HERE

Minnesota Vikings safety Harrison Smith is one of the NFL's hardest hitters. Perhaps it's due to his pregame ritual. Before games, Smith often has a hard time eating. So he uses a drink to give him a jolt of energy.

Before every game, Smith drinks a large shot glass of hot sauce. The spicy flavors help him get into the right zone for the game.

"It wakes me up," he said. "The hot sauce is mandatory."

LUCKY PENNY

Even coaches have superstitions. Once, before a big game, University of Alabama coach Nick Saban received a lucky penny from his daughter. Alabama won that game. Since then, his daughter has delivered a penny to the coach before every game.

CURSES AND JINXES

Even after a game begins, some teams are still up against bad luck and mind tricks. But are these concerns real or just myths?

FEELING BLUE

In the NFL, home teams usually wear dark jerseys. The Cowboys are the **exception**. They wear white at home games. And they often wear white jerseys on the road since their opponents wear dark colors.

The Dallas team won five Super Bowls wearing white jerseys. Fans began to believe the Cowboys' blue jerseys were bad luck. Other teams began wearing white at home so that Dallas would wear their blue tops.

While it may not be a real jinx, the Cowboys' record makes you wonder. By October 2021, the team had 72 wins, 76 losses, and 1 tie in their blue jerseys during the regular season.

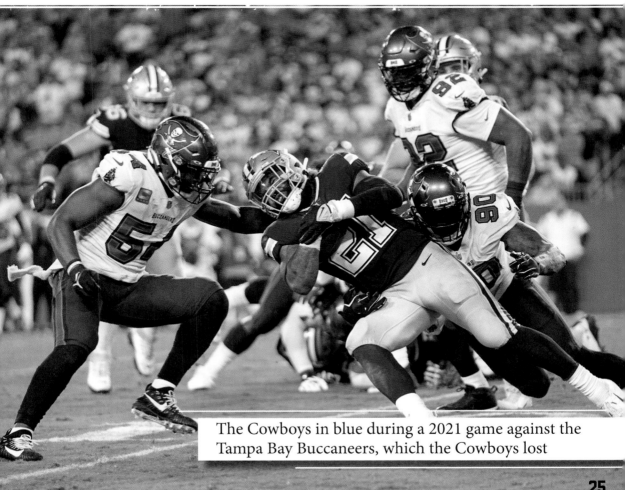

The Cowboys in blue during a 2021 game against the Tampa Bay Buccaneers, which the Cowboys lost

THE MADDEN CURSE

Each year Electronic Arts (EA) selects a football player—or two—to appear on the cover of their video game series *Madden NFL*. You'd think that being the face of the video game would be a great honor, but for many players, it's cause for concern. Some believe that being selected brings a player bad luck. They might have a bad season or an injury in the future.

Is it true? Who knows? But some players have had some pretty bad luck after appearing on the cover. Quarterback Daunte Culpepper appeared on the 2002 *Madden NFL* cover, which was released in 2001. During the 2001 season, he missed the last five weeks of the season because of a knee injury.

Daunte Culpepper

On the other hand, after appearing on the 2013 *Madden NFL* cover, wide receiver Calvin Johnson went on to have a great 2012 season. That season he set an NFL record of 1,964 receiving yards.

THE KIRK CURSE

Kirk Cousins is a solid NFL quarterback. But he has a unique statistic that makes him bad luck for opponents. No playoff team that has lost to Cousins in the regular season has ever gone to the Super Bowl.

Cousins has played against some pretty good teams. That list includes the Packers, the Cowboys, the Eagles, and the Steelers. So when an NFL team sees Cousins's team on their schedule, they should be worried.

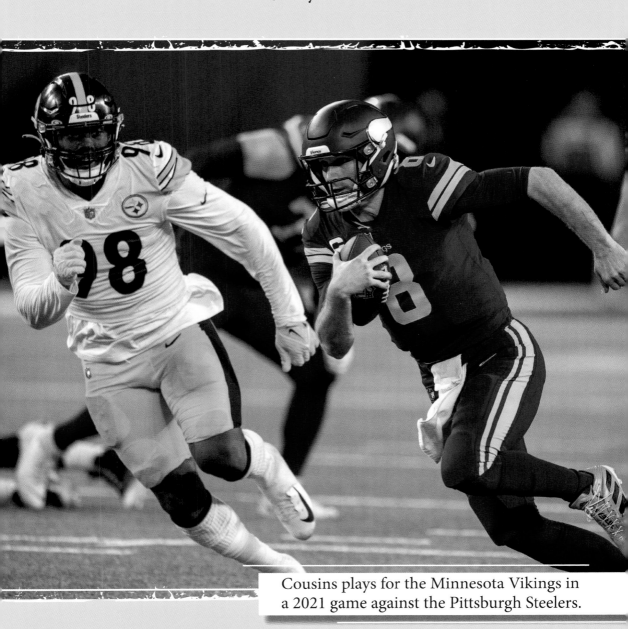

Cousins plays for the Minnesota Vikings in a 2021 game against the Pittsburgh Steelers.

GLOSSARY

alumni (uh-LUM-nahy)—a graduate of a college

cleat (KLEET)—a shoe with small tips on the bottom to help football players stop or turn quickly

elaborate (i-LAB-ur-it)—complicated and detailed

exception (ik-SEP-shuhn)—something that is treated differently

fumble (FUHM-buhl)—when a player drops the ball or it is knocked out of their hands by another player

Hail Mary (HAYL MER-ee)—a play during which the quarterback throws the ball deep toward the end zone in the hope that one of the team's receivers will catch it

host (HOHST)—providing things needed for an event, such as a game

throne (THROHN)—a special chair, usually used by someone important, like a king

READ MORE

Flynn, Brendan. *The Genius Kid's Guide to Pro Football.* Mendota Heights, MN: North Star Editions, 2022.

Lowe, Alexander. *G.O.A.T. Football Running Backs.* Minneapolis: Lerner Publications, 2023.

Zweig, Eric. *It's a Numbers Game! Football.* Washington, DC: National Geographic Partners, LLC, 2022.

INTERNET SITES

Go Noodle: NFL Play 60
gonoodle.com/tags/ZwmZ5Y/nfl-play-60

Kiddle: College Football Facts for Kids
kids.kiddle.co/College_football

Play Football: Discover FLAG Football
playfootball.nfl.com/parents/discover-flag-football/

INDEX

ABOUT THE AUTHOR

Elliott Smith is a freelance writer, editor, and author. He has covered a wide variety of subjects, including sports, entertainment, and travel, for newspapers, magazines, and websites. He has written a nonfiction book about the Washington Nationals and a children's book about Bryce Harper. He lives in the Washington, DC, area with his wife and two children.